Contents

NOCTURNAL ANIMALS

Wolves are nocturnal animals.

When you go to sleep at night, some animals are just waking up. These are **nocturnal** animals. They sleep in the daytime and are **active** at night.

Some animals are nocturnal because they live in hot places. They are active at night when it is cooler.

Some animals come out at night when it is easier to **hunt** for food.

Leopards often hunt at night.

This sloth sleeps in the daytime.

Some animals come out at night when it is safer. They sleep in the daytime so that other animals can't find them and eat them.

BATS

Bats usually live in caves and trees. Bats spend most of the day sleeping. Some bats live by themselves and others live in groups.

Bats are active at night when it is easier to hunt for food.

Most bats feed on insects. Bats hunt for insects by making a **high-pitched** beeping noise.

Bats use an echo to find food.

When the noise hits an insect it makes an **echo**. Bats can tell how far away the insect is by how quickly the echo travels back to them.

A bat can eat over one thousand insects in an hour!

AYE-AYES

Aye-ayes spend most of their lives in trees. They hardly ever come down to the ground.

Aye-ayes (say *eye-eyes*) live in tall trees. They sleep all day in a nest made of leaves and branches.

Aye-ayes spend most of the night looking for food. They eat insects, fruit, nuts and leaves. Their big eyes help them to see in the dark.

Aye-ayes have long fingers and sharp claws to stop them falling out of trees.

OWLS

Most owls live in trees. They sleep on branches in the daytime. Owls close their eyes when they are asleep.

At night, owls hunt for food. They eat birds, rabbits, mice and insects.

Owls can see and hear very well. This helps them to find food in the dark.

Owls have soft feathers on the edge of their wings. This helps them to fly quietly so they can sneak up on animals when they are hunting.

POSSUMS

Possums live in trees. They sleep during the daytime. This helps them to stay safe from animals like foxes and cats.

Possums come out at night to look for food.
They mostly eat plants and insects.

BADGERS

Badgers make several entrances to their home.

Badgers live under the ground. They dig tunnels with rooms. They sleep in one of the rooms during the daytime.

Badgers have long claws to help them dig.

Badgers live near trees and rivers because the ground is soft for digging. They dig to find food.

Badgers come out at night to look for food. They eat hundreds of worms every night.

Badgers use their strong sense of smell and hearing to help them find food.

Badgers also eat nuts, berries and other small animals like rabbits.

NOCTURNAL HOUSES

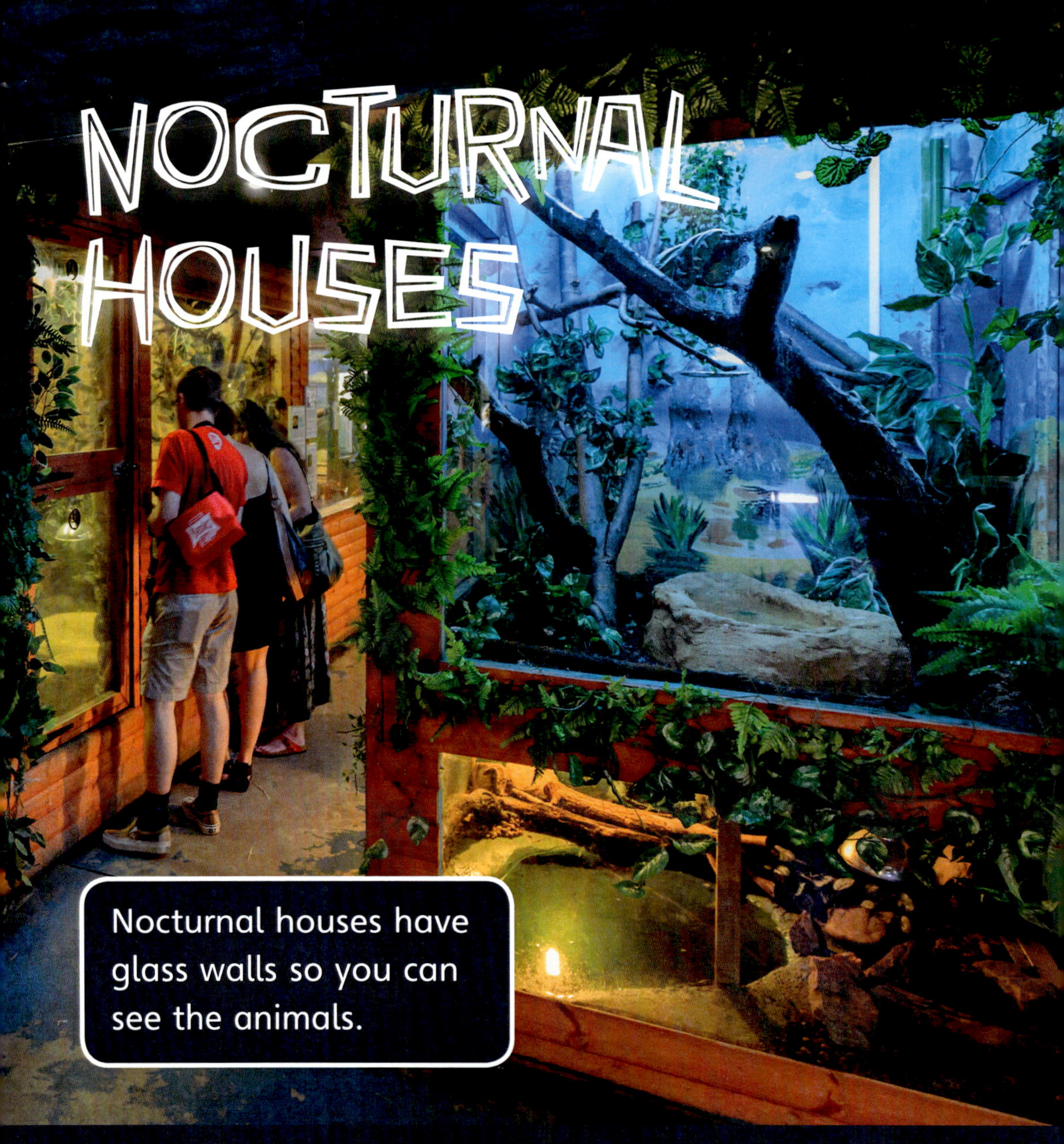

Nocturnal houses have glass walls so you can see the animals.

Where can you see nocturnal animals if they are only active at night? Try a nocturnal house at the zoo. It's a special building for nocturnal animals.

The lights in a nocturnal house are **dim** during the daytime. The animals think it is night. This means you can see them when they are awake!

GLOSSARY

active	moving around and doing things
dim	not a strong light
echo	noise that comes back
high-pitched	when a sound is high, like a scream
hunt	to chase animals for food
nocturnal	active during the night, not during the day
special	not ordinary or usual